GREAT
EVENTS

THAT CHANGED THE WORLD

ILLUSTRATED BY BRIAN DELF

WRITTEN BY RICHARD PLATT

DK PUBLISHING, INC.

A DK PUBLISHING BOOK

Senior Art Editor Dorian Spencer Davies
Senior Editor John C. Miles
U.S. Editor Camela Decaire
Senior Managing Art Editor Peter Bailey
Managing Editor Sarah Phillips
Production Charlotte Traill
DTP Designer Karen Nettelfield

First American Edition, 1997
2 4 6 8 10 9 7 5 3 1

Published in the United States by
DK Publishing, Inc.
95 Madison Avenue
New York, New York 10016

Published in Great Britain by Dorling Kindersley Ltd.

A catalog record for this book is available
from the Library of Congress

ISBN 0-7894-2030-9

Reproduced by Dot Gradations, Essex
Printed and bound in Italy by A. Mondadori Editore, Verona

CONTENTS

INTRODUCTION
4

THE GREAT PYRAMID
6

ALEXANDER THE GREAT
8

THE ROMAN EMPIRE
10

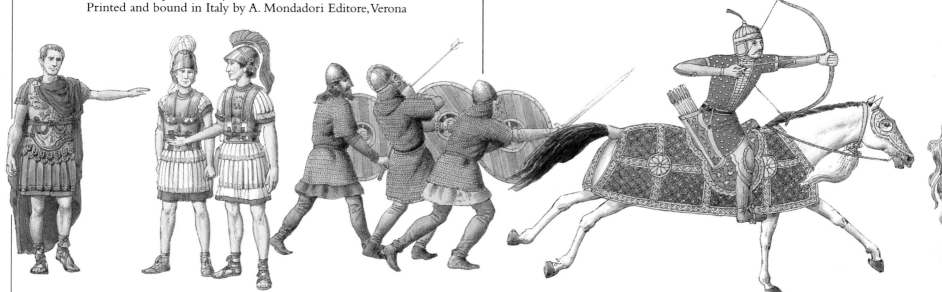

THE VIKINGS
12

THE FIRST CRUSADE
14

THE HUNDRED YEARS WAR
16

THE FALL OF THE AZTECS
18

THE MOGUL DYNASTY
20

THE REVOLUTIONARY WAR
22

THE FRENCH REVOLUTION
24

REVOLUTION IN RUSSIA
26

WORLD WAR I
28

WORLD WAR II
30

INDEX AND
ACKNOWLEDGMENTS
32

Introduction

The past is like a beautiful and valuable book written in many different languages. A few of its pages are plain enough for anyone to read, understand, and enjoy. Many, though, are a challenge to decipher. Other pages are missing altogether. The book tells a weird and wonderful mixture of stories. Some chapters tell of the everyday lives of past civilizations, others of extraordinary adventures and terrible battles. And between the chapters there is sometimes a picture, full of fascinating detail. Even the colors are as bright and fresh as the day they were painted.

The Egyptian civilization would appear in one of these pictures. Egypt's dry climate has preserved every detail of ancient Egyptian life with the clarity of a photograph. Other African civilizations have not fared so well. Their treasures have not survived the heat and the humidity of the rain forest. If the past really were a book, the pages of many cultures would be crumbling and mildewed.

The great book of history would include vivid descriptions of heroes from the past – friends and enemies writing about their victories. Portraits could even be stamped on coins tucked down the spine. Alexander the Great is one such hero. His personality comes across so clearly you can almost see him.

Sometimes, though, it's not an individual person who would capture your imagination, but a whole people. The story of the Romans is an engrossing one. Fortunately, their obsession with recording detail has ensured a very clear picture of their daily lives.

The Viking people left their mark, too, but in quite a different way. Their pages of history would be written in ancient runes (magic letters). Some historians peering at these inscriptions insist these people were fierce warriors. But others read the runes differently, and tell a tale of intrepid explorers, peaceful settlers and colonists.

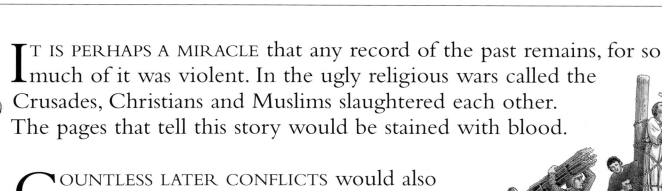

IT IS PERHAPS A MIRACLE that any record of the past remains, for so much of it was violent. In the ugly religious wars called the Crusades, Christians and Muslims slaughtered each other. The pages that tell this story would be stained with blood.

COUNTLESS LATER CONFLICTS would also appear as ugly gashes on our book. One chapter would have to describe a century of conflict – the Hundred Years War – that ripped through Europe 700 years ago. It would have at least one missing page – twisted into a taper, this page lit a fire that burned France's heroine Joan of Arc.

NOT EVERY CULTURE from the past has had need of writing. When the Aztec people of Mexico recorded their history, they used glyphs – little drawings. (A stranger to this amazing world might be forgiven for suddenly slamming the book shut. Aztec cities echo with the cries of human sacrifices.) The Aztec glyphs stop suddenly in mid-story, though; the end of their short tale is written in the Spanish language of their foreign conquerors.

WHAT SORT OF COVER would protect this great book of the past? If it were bound in India three or four centuries ago, it would be fine indeed. Under the Mogul emperors who ruled India, handicrafts flourished. Lavish decoration was fashionable – so jewels and precious metals might decorate the carefully tooled bookbinding.

EVEN IN A RAGGED cardboard binding, the stories of revolution – in the United States, France, or Russia – would make fascinating reading. These might begin in the neat handwriting of a smug official, and end in a hurried scrawl. Revolutionaries seizing power violently have little time for neatness. Nor do they always write the truth. After the Russian revolution, the country's new rulers hurried to change history; holes in pictures show where disgraced leaders once stood.

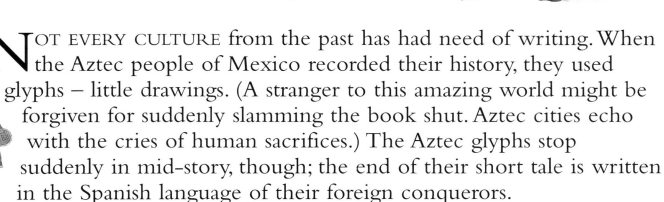

OUR BOOK OF THE PAST would end with world wars. Mud from the trenches would cake the chapter on World War I, the bottom of its last page inscribed with the moving words, "This war ended all wars."

SADLY, THE FINAL chapter of our book would disprove these words. World War II could have an even more frightening treatment, glowing with the green light of nuclear radiation.

The Great Pyramid

THE VALLEY OF THE NILE RIVER winds through the red African desert like a wide black ribbon. Five thousand years ago, the people who farmed its rich soil formed a great nation called Egypt. They were ruled by powerful kings known as pharaohs, who lived like gods. The ancient Egyptians believed in life after death and their rulers planned for it in style. At Giza, on the banks of the Nile near modern-day Cairo, a pharaoh named Khufu built a fantastic tomb 44 centuries ago. It is still the largest burial monument anywhere in the world.

Oxen pulling plow

LIFE ON THE LAND, 3000 BC

When the Nile flooded each year, it coated the fields with fertile mud. Little rain fell and the farmers needed the flood water, so everybody got involved in building irrigation ditches and canals. This common purpose helped bond Egyptian society together. Barley, wheat, and beans grew in the hot climate.

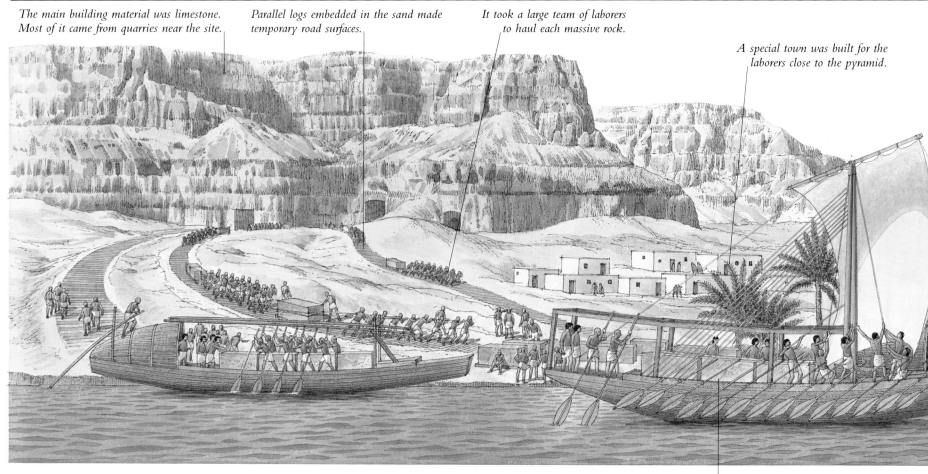

The main building material was limestone. Most of it came from quarries near the site.

Parallel logs embedded in the sand made temporary road surfaces.

It took a large team of laborers to haul each massive rock.

A special town was built for the laborers close to the pyramid.

The Nile was a highway: ships drifted to the sea with the current and sailed back. Granite for Khufu's burial chamber, for example, was brought from Aswan, 600 miles (950 km) upriver.

PROJECT PYRAMID

Khufu (also known by his Greek name, Cheops) ruled from 2589-2566 BC. The awesome task of building his pyramid was begun while he was still alive. Workers used two million stone blocks. Most weighed around two and a half tons, but some were much bigger. Construction took about 20 years.

Work went on all year round, but the busiest time was during the summer, when the Nile flooded the fields and farm workers were made to help with the building.

Khufu's body was carried to his funeral on a boat-shaped sled.

Priest

The number of mourners at a funeral showed how important the dead person was.

Like all the pharaohs, Khufu was buried with a collection of furniture, foods, and other objects he might need in the afterlife.

Living servants may have been sealed in the pyramid with Khufu, especially if they knew about the secret traps and passages designed to protect the pyramid from thieves.

A PHARAOH'S FUNERAL

Egyptians saw death as a journey from life to afterlife. In later ages, they invented a technique for preserving the appearance of life in the dead. Some of these preserved bodies still exist – they are called mummies. When Khufu died though, this wasn't possible, so he probably had a carved death mask.

If farmers watered their fields by hand, they could have two harvests every year.

Threshed wheat

Egyptian carpenters made holes in wood by rotating a flint point with a bow.

Scribes were government officials who could read and write, unlike ordinary people. One of their jobs was to measure fields and figure out how much tax people owed.

PAYMENT IN KIND
People paid taxes according to the size of their land and the number of animals they owned. Egyptians did not use money – they paid for everything by barter (exchange). Taxes financed those who did not work on the land, such as the pharaoh, his family and officials, priests, and their servants.

Oxen trampled the wheat to separate the dry husks from the grains inside. This process, called threshing, was carried out on a threshing floor – a hard, level surface inside a low wall.

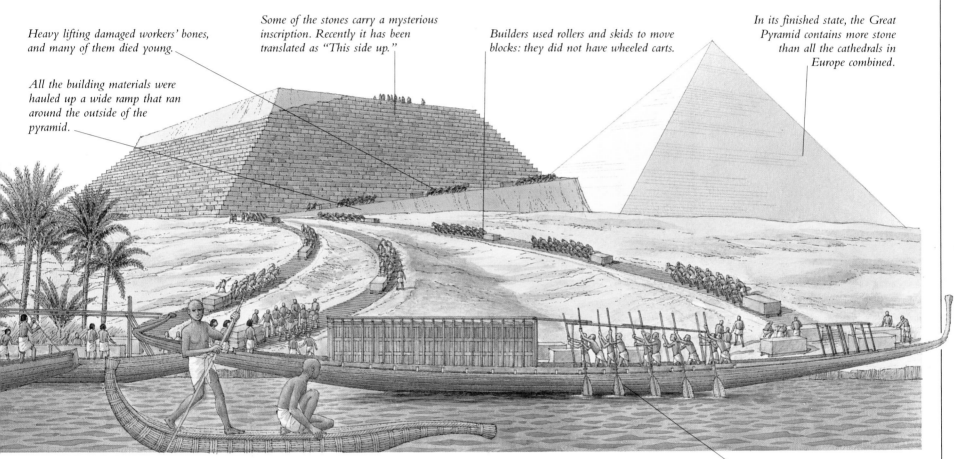

Heavy lifting damaged workers' bones, and many of them died young.

Some of the stones carry a mysterious inscription. Recently it has been translated as "This side up."

Builders used rollers and skids to move blocks: they did not have wheeled carts.

In its finished state, the Great Pyramid contains more stone than all the cathedrals in Europe combined.

All the building materials were hauled up a wide ramp that ran around the outside of the pyramid.

THE LAST JOURNEY, 2566 BC
Buried in the sand beside the Great Pyramid was Khufu's funeral barge, made from rare, fragrant cedar, held together with hemp rope. Wood carvers shaped the frame so it looked like the traditional reed boats used for transportation on the Nile. Some experts believe this vessel carried Khufu on his last journey, while others think it was placed near him so he could use it in the afterlife. In any case, when archaeologists dug the boat up in 1954, it still smelled strongly of cedar.

Powered by ten oarsmen, Khufu's boat was 70 ft (21 m) long. Fresh palm leaves inside the cabin roof kept his body cool.

By Tutankhamen's time, masons were raiding the pyramids for stone to use in new buildings.

A fabulous gold death mask covered the face of Tutankhamen's mummy.

ANCIENT MONUMENTS
Egyptians continued to bury their rulers in pyramids for another 800 years, but the Nile civilization flourished for much longer. Khufu's pyramid was more than twelve centuries old, and was considered an ancient relic, by the time of the boy-pharaoh Tutankhamen, who was born in 1341 BC.

GRAVE SECRETS, 1323 BC
When Tutankhamen died, at age 18, he was buried in an underground tomb in the Valley of the Kings, 315 miles (510 km) from the Great Pyramid. His grave survived intact until the twentieth century. From its treasures, and those of other tombs, we know more about death rituals in ancient Egypt than about daily life.

Alexander the Great

THERE IS AN OLD GREEK COIN showing the warrior king Alexander, the first leader to be nicknamed "the Great." The coin was stamped from plundered gold 23 centuries ago. Alexander looks proud on the coin, which isn't surprising since he built a gigantic empire, stretching from Greece to India and Egypt, in just 11 years. With loyal troops he won great victories – and never lost a battle. He also founded 70 cities, several of which were given the name Alexandria. Alexander believed he was a god, and demanded hero worship. He was hungry for power and used power ruthlessly. But he died – probably from heavy drinking – at the age of just 33.

2. BATTLE OF ISSOS, 333 BC

Alexander wanted to carry out his father's plan to conquer Persia. This was the empire of King Darius III, and stretched from Turkey to India in the east and Egypt in the south. The invasion began in 334 BC, and soon Alexander controlled much of the western Persian empire. The following year Alexander and Darius fought at Issos (now in Turkey). Though heavily outnumbered, Alexander's well-trained troops won the battle. Darius fled, leaving his wife, mother, and children at Alexander's mercy.

Alexander realized Bucephalus was frightened of his shadow and calmed him by turning him to face the sun.

Alexander led the charge across a river that separated his soldiers from the Persians.

King Darius III

1. BIRTH OF A LEGEND, 356 BC

Born in 356 BC, Alexander was the son of the Macedonian king, Philip II. He grew up brave and strong, and was a skilled rider. When he was 12 he was given a fine horse, called Bucephalus, which no adult could control. On his father's death in 336 BC, Alexander became king of Macedonia – and of Greece, which Philip had conquered in 334.

3. SIEGE OF TYRE, 332 BC

From his victory at Issos, Alexander marched south, conquering more Persian lands. Many cities surrendered without a fight, but capturing Tyre took seven months. When the city finally fell in July 332 BC, his troops brutally slaughtered the men and enslaved the women.

Siege tower

The people of Tyre used burning ships to set light to the siege towers that Alexander's troops had built.

Alexander finally defeated Darius's armies at Gaugamela in 331 BC.

Pella

Ankyra

Gordion

Perge

Tarsos

Issos 333 BC

Gaugamela 331 BC

Arbela

Thapsakos

Byblos
Tyre

Damascus

Babylon

Tyre 332 BC

Alexandria

Pelusium

Parraetonium

Memphis

Siwa

During his time in Egypt, Alexander sent an expedition to find the reason for the Nile River's annual flood.

4. CONQUEST IN EGYPT, 332 BC

From Tyre, Alexander marched on to conquer Egypt in November 332 BC. The Egyptian people, who hated their Persian rulers, welcomed him as a pharaoh – a god king. The adoration went to Alexander's head: he, too, began to believe he was a god. Alexander stayed in Egypt until April 331, and founded the city of Alexandria. Meanwhile, his enemy Darius, who had not been completely defeated, was putting together a new army.

8. DEATH IN BABYLON, 323 BC

Alexander's short but astonishing life ended in 323 BC. He went to a banquet in Babylon, and then continued to drink late into the night. After drinking over three quarts of wine, he collapsed. Ten days later on June 13, he died. He was taken to Egypt and buried in a gold coffin in Alexandria.

Poisoned wine may have killed Alexander.

At Hydaspes the elephants advanced in a line, as a mobile fortress. But under attack the line was broken. In the retreat many Indians were stampeded.

The elephant cavalry trampled the enemy underfoot, and used tusks and trunks to drive a way forward.

5. EAST TO INDIA, 326 BC

The armies of Darius and Alexander met in 331 BC at Gaugamela (now in Iraq). Darius was defeated, but he escaped, only to be murdered by a governor who wanted to be king in his place. Alexander was now "Lord of Asia," but he wanted to earn the title. He marched east, meeting fierce resistance from the Indian people. At the Hydaspes River, in June 326 BC, his army won a key battle against soldiers mounted on 200 elephants. Alexander continued to battle his way across India, but his troops were growing weary. They had been fighting for eight years and wanted to return home. Alexander tried to rally them with a speech, but failed. Reluctantly he agreed to end his campaign.

Boukephala was named after Alexander's horse, which died here of old age.

Samarkand

Drapsaka

Boukephala

Taxila

Kabul

Zadracarta

Susia

Hydaspes, 326 BC

Tehran

Alexandria of Aria (Herat)

Hamadan

7. BACK TO SUSA, 324 BC

On Alexander's return from India in 324, there was a feast at Susa to celebrate his conquest of the Persian empire. In a mass wedding, Alexander and 80 officers took Persian brides.

Prophthasia

Kandahar

Susa

Persepolis

Alexander hoped that taking a Persian bride would bind the Macedonians and the Persians together.

Alexandria

Pattala

ALEXANDER THE LEGEND

While he lived, Alexander was already a legend. After his death, the stories about him became even more fantastic. Now, more than 2,000 years later, fact and myth are impossible to separate. All we can be sure of is what is revealed by coins and stone inscriptions that date from Alexander's time.

Alexander earned the loyalty of his men because he suffered the same hardships as they did.

6. TREK THROUGH THE DESERT, 325 BC

In 325 BC Alexander's armies began their long journey home. Some of his troops returned to Susa, the Persian capital, by sea. Alexander led the rest back overland. It was a terrible mistake. Their march became an ordeal of thirst and scorching heat. To add to their torment, a sudden cloudburst turned into a flood, and many were drowned. Sandstorms blinded them, and they lost their way. Starving soldiers slaughtered their pack animals and ate the meat raw. Alexander led 85,000 people into the desert, but only 25,000 survived.

The Roman Empire

Horatius

ACCORDING TO LEGEND, one of the world's greatest civilizations was founded by orphaned twins named Romulus and Remus. Set afloat on the Tiber River in what is now central Italy, they were rescued by a she-wolf, who suckled them like cubs. When they grew into men, they built a settlement at the spot where they had been abandoned. They argued violently however, and Romulus killed Remus. The new city was named Rome after Romulus, and he became its first king in about 750 BC. This city eventually controlled a vast empire that included most of western Europe.

HORATIUS SAVES THE CITY OF ROME, 509 BC

The Romans expelled a cruel king named Tarquin. He returned, but his only access was by a small bridge. Three soldiers defended it while engineers cut its supports. Two fled, but the last, Horatius Cocles, guarded it until it collapsed.

Few elephants survived their journey across the mountains.

Hannibal

WAR WITH CARTHAGE

Rome fought a series of wars with the North African empire of Carthage. During one war, Carthage threatened to attack from Spain.

Rome controlled the Mediterranean Sea, so the enemy general, Hannibal, marched overland with 40,000 foot soldiers, cavalry, and elephants. During the five-month journey,

he fought hostile tribes and crossed both the Pyrenees and the Alps. It took Rome 17 years to defeat Hannibal.

ROMAN TRIUMPHS, 146 BC

Rome finally destroyed Carthage in 146 BC. By then, other wars had given Rome control of Greece and most of the eastern Mediterranean.

Julius Caesar in Gaul

Siege tower

THE AGE OF CAESAR

Before long, Rome ruled the Mediterranean world. Its politicians became greedy and ambitious. The most ambitious of all was Julius

Caesar. Under his command, Roman soldiers conquered Gaul (France). But Caesar's enemies had been plotting against him, and his return in 49 BC led to civil war.

Caesar's troops helped him defeat his rivals. But Caesar had become a dictator, ruling on his own and naming his adopted son Octavian as his heir.

On March 15, 44 BC, Caesar was attacked by a group of enemies led by two senators, Brutus and Cassius. They stabbed him to death.

Hadrian's wall was 12 ft (3.5 m) high.

By Roman times, the Pyramids were already ancient.

NORTHERN BORDER

Roman armies had invaded England in AD 44; 80 years later, Emperor Hadrian built a long wall to guard England's northern frontier.

PAX ROMANA, AD 117

By AD 117, Rome controlled most of the world as Europeans knew it. They did this with a highly trained army. Volunteer soldiers (legionaries) conquered a new territory, policed it, and retired there. The Romans ruled by force, and the resulting stability was known as *pax Romana* (Roman peace).

SOUTHWESTERN FRONTIER

Roman rule extended southwest to Egypt. The Nile valley supplied grain, and luxuries such as wild beasts, used to fight gladiators.

A meeting of the Senate

Prisoners were taken to Rome as slaves.

THE ROMAN REPUBLIC

After Tarquin's defeat, the Romans made their city a republic (a state ruled by its citizens). In annual elections, they chose two leaders, called consuls, who together ruled the city and led its armies. Three hundred old men of patrician (noble) families advised the consuls. This group was known as the Senate.

CONQUERING ARMIES

Rome's well-organized armies captured the surrounding states, then lands that were farther away. A network of military roads allowed soldiers to travel wherever they were needed, and by 275 BC, Rome controlled all of present-day Italy. The Roman conquests created many enemies, however.

Famous gladiators were celebrities like today's rock stars.

Soldiers lined a long road called the Appian Way with 6,000 crucified slaves.

SLAVERY AND REVOLT

Prisoners captured in these wars became slaves; some worked the land in place of farmers who had gone to war; others served wealthy Romans. At one time, slaves outnumbered free men 3 to 1, and revolts were common. Some slaves, called gladiators, were forced to provide entertainment by fighting each other to death. One of them, a gladiator named Spartacus, led a famous slave revolt in 73 BC.

Rebel slaves were captured and crucified (tied to a cross until they died). Sometimes thousands of slaves were crucified at one time.

Octavian assumed the title Augustus (venerable).

Nero even drank a traditional charioteer's potion of boar dung.

THE FIRST EMPEROR, 27 BC–AD 14

After a period of unrest, Octavian took control. The Senate made him Rome's first emperor, ending the Republic and giving him total power. Nevertheless, he ruled wisely. The arts flourished, and many new buildings were constructed.

CRUELTY AND CORRUPTION, AD 54-68

Nero, the fifth emperor, was a vain, cruel man who had his mother and wife murdered. When half of Rome burned down, he blamed the Christians, then rebuilt a third of the city as his palace. Nero's love of chariot racing – a Roman obsession – kept him in power, but eventually he was overthrown.

BARBARIANS ARRIVE, 200

Barbarian hordes began to invade the empire when leadership squabbles and civil wars had weakened it from inside.

Led by King Alaric, the Visigoths (descendants of a Scandinavian race) attacked the city of Rome in 410. Later, other barbarian tribes such as the Vandals did the same.

THE FALL OF ROME, 476

The last emperor was deposed by barbarians in AD 476, and after more than 1,000 years, Roman rule crumbled. To see its legacy, however, just look at a calendar – we still use the Roman 26-letter alphabet, and 365-day calendar. The month of August is even named after Augustus.

The Vikings

A HARDY RACE OF PEOPLE settled in Denmark, Norway, and Sweden some 4,500 years ago. Their skill at ironworking helped them flourish, and by AD 700, there were so many people in the coastal towns and villages that some of them set sail in search of new lands. Armed with sharp iron weapons, and transported in superbly built boats, these raiders made many daring attacks on foreign coasts. For this reason, they became known as pirates, or, in their own language, "vikingr."

A skilled man could take a month to make a blade.

Each wooden shield had an iron disk, or boss, in the middle to protect the warrior's hand.

MEN OF IRON

Metalworking techniques were vital to the Vikings, since iron axes could cut down trees to provide wood for building and fuel. Farmers then grew crops on the cleared land. In addition to axes and weapons, smiths made locks, pots, and rivets for ships. They also worked other metals, such as bronze and gold.

Vikings gave their favorite swords names, such as "Leg-Biter."

Monks founded a monastery on Lindisfarne in 635.

PIRATE RAIDERS

Vikings, like all early sailors, tried to stay near land; when they did cross the sea, they used the sun and stars to navigate. On arrival, they could haul their shallow, light ships onto a beach. At the end of the 8th century, the Vikings began attacking England.

LINDISFARNE ATTACKED, 793

Early raiders landed on the island of Lindisfarne, off the northeastern coast of England, and raided the monastery there. To the pagan Vikings, monasteries were easy targets; many of them were storehouses of precious religious treasures, and they were often left undefended.

Novgorod resembled a Wild West town.

EASTERN EXPLOITS

Crossing the Baltic Sea, the Vikings penetrated the area that is now Russia. A web of rivers allowed them to sail inland on trading expeditions. At major junctions such as Novgorod, they built towns that became large trade centers. The local name for Vikings – Rus – may be the root of the word Russia.

To negotiate shallow inland rivers, merchants used boats that were smaller and lighter than the raiding longships.

PUSHING SOUTHWARD

Rivers linking the Baltic and Black seas led to Constantinople, where weapons, fur, and slaves were traded for silver.

New Viking Christians gather in prayer.

GROWING AND CHANGING

Wherever Vikings settled, they absorbed the culture. When they married local women, for example, their children spoke a language that took words from both parents. Because most countries they settled in had a Latin-based language, Latin letters soon replaced Viking writing. But the greatest influence on the Vikings was religious – although they had always worshiped pagan gods (and much of our knowledge about them comes from their pagan relics), they became Christians.

To celebrate important events and people, the Vikings erected memorial stones in public places. The symbols on these stones paid tribute to qualities like bravery and strength.

Vikings valued women for their wisdom.

Nails made from iron and wood held Viking raider ships together.

People captured in raids worked as slaves.

Vikings carved fierce beasts on the prows of their ships to frighten their enemies.

SPEEDY SHIPS

After centuries of living by the sea, Vikings became expert shipbuilders. Early Viking ships carried timber, millstones, livestock, and wool. These vessels were large and broad, and powered with a single square sail, so they were quite slow. Viking raiders, however, had ships built for them that were narrow and long, so they could reach speeds of up to 11 knots (13 mph/20 kmh). Powered mainly by sails, they also had oars on either side to make them even faster when necessary.

Fortified military camp

Making bread

HIT AND RUN, 844

From England, the raiders turned their sights south. They attacked Seville in 844 and Paris in 845, then ransacked the Mediterranean. Initially, they would arrive in a new place, stay for the summer, then leave. Often, the locals bribed them to go, so without having to fight, they sailed home laden with booty.

SETTLING DOWN

By the mid-9th century, the raiders were settling in the places they attacked. Where no towns existed, they fortified military camps, brought in seeds and plows – and their families – and formed communities. By 900, Vikings had settled in eastern England and created a trade center in Dublin.

Wherever they settled, the Vikings built characteristic long dwellings.

Most men wore a simple wool tunic and pants.

HEADING WEST, 870

Viking adventurers established colonies in Iceland, farming the island from about 870. A century later, they settled in Greenland.

DISCOVERING NEW LANDS, 986

According to legend, a Viking ship reached present-day Canada about 986, 500 years before Columbus, when it blew off course from Greenland. For a short time, Vikings had a colony there called Vinland (Wineland). Experts aren't sure where this was, but Viking artifacts have been found in Newfoundland.

Their skill at metalworking helped the Vikings settle new lands. With iron axes, they chopped down trees, notching and fitting the resulting logs to build lots of new houses.

Vikings believed they went straight to heaven if they died fighting.

An English arrow killed Harald the Ruthless.

THE FINAL RAID, 1066

Marrying local women may have diluted Viking blood, but in England, only spilling it put an end to the Viking age. In 1066, a Viking army led by Harald the Ruthless, king of Norway, landed on the Humber River, but the English army defeated him at nearby Stamford Bridge. The celebrations did not last long. Less than three weeks later, William of Normandy and his force of 10,000 men landed at Hastings on the southeastern coast, and defeated the battle-weary English troops.

LASTING LEGACY

Viking influence is still with us, in law, literature, and in words that have Viking roots, such as bread, sky, and Thursday (after the god Thor).

The First Crusade

"GOD WILLS IT!" was a battle cry for thousands of Christians across Europe in 1095. They believed God wanted them to capture Jerusalem and the Holy Land from the Turkish Muslims. In fact, Jerusalem had been ruled by Muslims since 637, but they were Arab Muslims, who tolerated Christians. In 1071 though, the city was seized by Turks, who wanted Christians out. As a result, hundreds of people joined a pilgrimage (holy journey) to the Holy Land. These warrior pilgrims sewed crosses on their clothes; the French word for cross is *croix*, so people spoke of going on *croisades*. In English, this became Crusades.

Pope Urban II

CALL TO ARMS, 1095

By 1095, Turkish Muslims were attacking Christians in the Holy Land and threatening Constantinople (Istanbul), the Byzantine capital. The First Crusade was inspired by Pope Urban II, who called on European Christians to support the Byzantine emperor Alexius, leader of Christians in the east.

Emperor Alexius greets Peter the Hermit, who by this stage was leading the collected People's Crusades.

Turkish Muslims massacred most of the People's Crusaders.

CRUSADERS REACH CONSTANTINOPLE, 1096

In the summer of 1096, the People's Crusades reached Constantinople, where Emperor Alexius met them. Soon, eager for a fight, mobs broke away and raided the nearby countryside. Mistaking Christian villagers for Turks, they killed them in particularly cruel ways, spit-roasting their children alive.

MASSACRE AT CIBOTUS, 1096

The unruly army crossed the Bosporus (the narrow sea separating Europe and Asia), but at Cibotus (now Dinar, Turkey) they were ambushed by Muslims. Peter, who had returned to Constantinople for help, escaped. The next April, a wave of Crusader reinforcements arrived at Constantinople.

The Crusaders built high siege towers so they could attack the walled city.

The wooden siege towers were hung with damp hides to make them resistant to fire.

Holy men accompanied the Crusaders and regularly blessed their struggle.

THE GOAL IN SIGHT, 1099

The Crusaders marched south from Antioch to Jerusalem. On July 13, they launched their assault on the city and the Muslims who held it.

The Crusaders had huge catapults, which used coiled rope to smash a long bar up against a crossbeam. The resulting force could propel a heavy missile over the city walls.

THE FALL OF JERUSALEM

The Crusaders broke through within two days, killing every non-Christian they found. They did not even spare women and children. The unexpected victory convinced the Crusaders that God was on their side. Most returned home triumphant, but some stayed on along the eastern Mediterranean.

Peter the Hermit led ordinary citizens in a "People's Crusade."

THE FIRST WAVE

The Pope expected knights (rich noblemen) to join him, but of the 40,000 Crusaders, nine-tenths were common people. The Crusade did not begin as the Pope had planned. Before the knights were ready, rag-tag armies set off from several cities. One of these "People's Crusades" was led by a popular preacher called Peter the Hermit. Many pilgrims sold all their possessions to pay for the trip, which they knew would be difficult. Their faith helped them endure disease, hunger, and hardship.

Crusaders believed it was their holy duty to attack infidels (non-Christians). Some People's Crusades used this as justification for killing Jews or burning their houses.

SIEGE OF ANTIOCH, 1097

By October, the Crusaders had reached Antioch (now Antkya, Turkey). Unable to storm the city, they besieged it. For eight months, they waited outside the walls in terrible conditions, praying for surrender. News of the long siege reached Emperor Alexius on his way to Antioch from Constantinople – discouraged, he turned back. Finally, in June 1098, a Muslim armorer accepted a bribe to open a gate. The Crusaders rushed in and killed almost every Muslim in the city.

Just when they were most discouraged, the Crusaders discovered a holy relic – a lance they believed was used to spear Jesus. They saw this as a sign that they were fighting a just cause.

Muslim merchants eventually traded with the Crusaders.

Central rudder

Traders brought back silk, cotton, linen, damask, sugar, and oriental spices from the Arab world.

European sailors were quick to replace their steering oars with the better central rudders they saw on Muslim ships.

LATER CAMPAIGNS

Crusaders returned many times over the next 200 years, but never had the same success. By 1291, the Holy Land was again under Muslim rule.

A LASTING LEGACY

The Crusades brought a number of benefits. Christian groups that once fought each other joined forces against the Muslims. Once they were brought into contact, Christians and Muslims learned from one another. Trade also boomed. European ships that carried supplies to the east went back with luxury goods. The western world gained knowledge as well, especially of astronomy. So, four centuries after the Crusades began, Europeans crossed the Atlantic using instruments copied from the Arabs.

The Hundred Years War

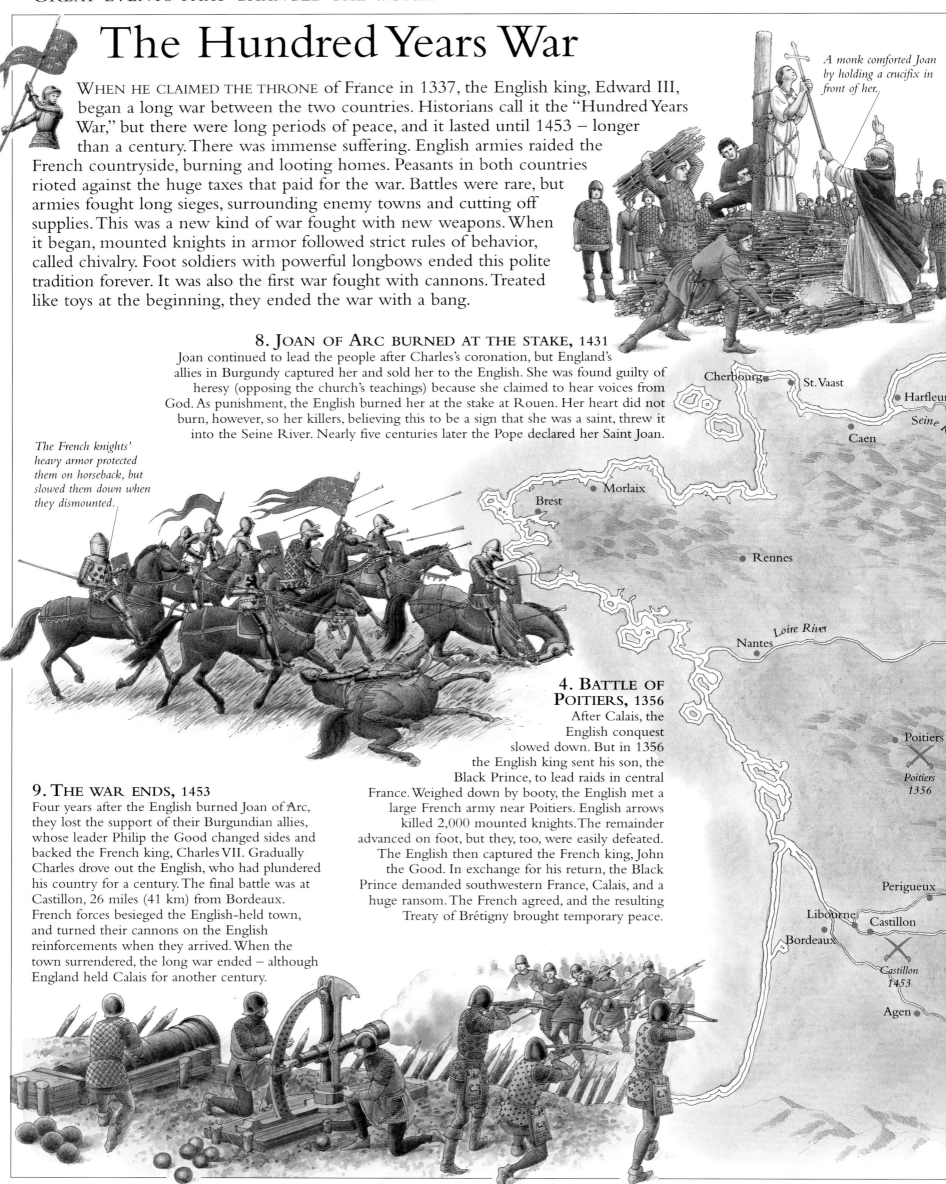

WHEN HE CLAIMED THE THRONE of France in 1337, the English king, Edward III, began a long war between the two countries. Historians call it the "Hundred Years War," but there were long periods of peace, and it lasted until 1453 – longer than a century. There was immense suffering. English armies raided the French countryside, burning and looting homes. Peasants in both countries rioted against the huge taxes that paid for the war. Battles were rare, but armies fought long sieges, surrounding enemy towns and cutting off supplies. This was a new kind of war fought with new weapons. When it began, mounted knights in armor followed strict rules of behavior, called chivalry. Foot soldiers with powerful longbows ended this polite tradition forever. It was also the first war fought with cannons. Treated like toys at the beginning, they ended the war with a bang.

A monk comforted Joan by holding a crucifix in front of her.

8. JOAN OF ARC BURNED AT THE STAKE, 1431
Joan continued to lead the people after Charles's coronation, but England's allies in Burgundy captured her and sold her to the English. She was found guilty of heresy (opposing the church's teachings) because she claimed to hear voices from God. As punishment, the English burned her at the stake at Rouen. Her heart did not burn, however, so her killers, believing this to be a sign that she was a saint, threw it into the Seine River. Nearly five centuries later the Pope declared her Saint Joan.

The French knights' heavy armor protected them on horseback, but slowed them down when they dismounted.

9. THE WAR ENDS, 1453
Four years after the English burned Joan of Arc, they lost the support of their Burgundian allies, whose leader Philip the Good changed sides and backed the French king, Charles VII. Gradually Charles drove out the English, who had plundered his country for a century. The final battle was at Castillon, 26 miles (41 km) from Bordeaux. French forces besieged the English-held town, and turned their cannons on the English reinforcements when they arrived. When the town surrendered, the long war ended – although England held Calais for another century.

4. BATTLE OF POITIERS, 1356
After Calais, the English conquest slowed down. But in 1356 the English king sent his son, the Black Prince, to lead raids in central France. Weighed down by booty, the English met a large French army near Poitiers. English arrows killed 2,000 mounted knights. The remainder advanced on foot, but they, too, were easily defeated. The English then captured the French king, John the Good. In exchange for his return, the Black Prince demanded southwestern France, Calais, and a huge ransom. The French agreed, and the resulting Treaty of Brétigny brought temporary peace.

Cherbourg • St. Vaast
Harfleur •
Caen •
Seine R.
Morlaix •
Brest •
Rennes •
Nantes
Loire River
Poitiers •
Poitiers 1356
Perigueux •
Libourne • Castillon
Bordeaux •
Castillon 1453
Agen •

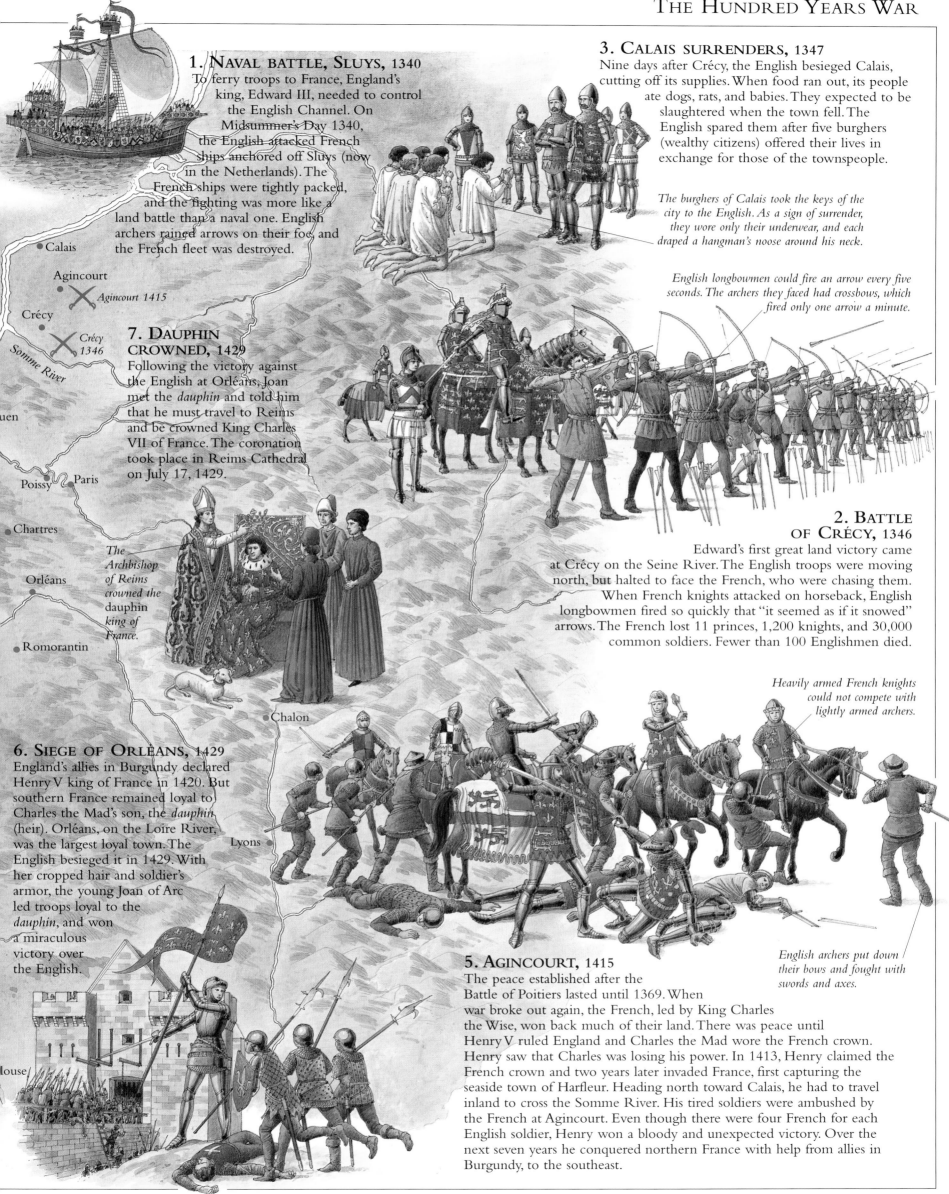

1. NAVAL BATTLE, SLUYS, 1340

To ferry troops to France, England's king, Edward III, needed to control the English Channel. On Midsummer's Day 1340, the English attacked French ships anchored off Sluys (now in the Netherlands). The French ships were tightly packed, and the fighting was more like a land battle than a naval one. English archers rained arrows on their foe, and the French fleet was destroyed.

3. CALAIS SURRENDERS, 1347

Nine days after Crécy, the English besieged Calais, cutting off its supplies. When food ran out, its people ate dogs, rats, and babies. They expected to be slaughtered when the town fell. The English spared them after five burghers (wealthy citizens) offered their lives in exchange for those of the townspeople.

The burghers of Calais took the keys of the city to the English. As a sign of surrender, they wore only their underwear, and each draped a hangman's noose around his neck.

English longbowmen could fire an arrow every five seconds. The archers they faced had crossbows, which fired only one arrow a minute.

7. DAUPHIN CROWNED, 1429

Following the victory against the English at Orléans, Joan met the *dauphin* and told him that he must travel to Reims and be crowned King Charles VII of France. The coronation took place in Reims Cathedral on July 17, 1429.

The Archbishop of Reims crowned the dauphin king of France.

2. BATTLE OF CRÉCY, 1346

Edward's first great land victory came at Crécy on the Seine River. The English troops were moving north, but halted to face the French, who were chasing them. When French knights attacked on horseback, English longbowmen fired so quickly that "it seemed as if it snowed" arrows. The French lost 11 princes, 1,200 knights, and 30,000 common soldiers. Fewer than 100 Englishmen died.

Heavily armed French knights could not compete with lightly armed archers.

6. SIEGE OF ORLÉANS, 1429

England's allies in Burgundy declared Henry V king of France in 1420. But southern France remained loyal to Charles the Mad's son, the *dauphin* (heir). Orléans, on the Loire River, was the largest loyal town. The English besieged it in 1429. With her cropped hair and soldier's armor, the young Joan of Arc led troops loyal to the *dauphin*, and won a miraculous victory over the English.

5. AGINCOURT, 1415

The peace established after the Battle of Poitiers lasted until 1369. When war broke out again, the French, led by King Charles the Wise, won back much of their land. There was peace until Henry V ruled England and Charles the Mad wore the French crown. Henry saw that Charles was losing his power. In 1413, Henry claimed the French crown and two years later invaded France, first capturing the seaside town of Harfleur. Heading north toward Calais, he had to travel inland to cross the Somme River. His tired soldiers were ambushed by the French at Agincourt. Even though there were four French for each English soldier, Henry won a bloody and unexpected victory. Over the next seven years he conquered northern France with help from allies in Burgundy, to the southeast.

English archers put down their bows and fought with swords and axes.

Map labels
Calais
Agincourt
Agincourt 1415
Crécy
Crécy 1346
Somme River
uen
Poissy
Paris
Chartres
Orléans
Romorantin
Chalon
Lyons
louse

The Fall of the Aztecs

PERCHING ON A CACTUS, an eagle ate a snake. To the Aztecs, then a wandering warrior tribe, this omen marked the place where they were to settle. So, in 1325, they founded the city of Tenochtitlan in the Valley of Mexico. Less than 200 years later, their empire stretched from the Atlantic to the Pacific. Ruled by the god-emperor Montezuma, the Aztecs enjoyed healthy trade, magnificent architecture, and complex feats of engineering such as aqueducts, canals, and causeways (raised roads). Then, in 1519, the Aztec world was suddenly destroyed by strangers from a distant land.

THE FIRST SETTLERS, 1325

The Aztec Empire began as an island community in Lake Texcoco. Land was scarce, so farmers drained lakeside marshes and built platform-mounted fields called *chinampas* for growing crops like corn. The Aztecs had not discovered the wheel, and had no pack animals, so boats were vital for transportation.

Royal Palace — *Great Pyramid* — *Priest*

MONTEZUMA'S COURT

The emperor, Montezuma II, lived at the heart of Tenochtitlan in a 300-room palace adjoining the main place of worship, the Great Pyramid.

From here he controlled the nobles and priests who ruled his empire. Priests were especially important since the Aztec people worshiped sun gods, and believed that without

the nourishment of human blood, the sun would stop shining. To mark one religious festival, priests stripped the skin from sacrificial victims and wore it as clothing for 20 days.

On top of huge, stepped pyramids, priests killed their sacrifices by tearing open their chest with a stone knife and plucking out their heart. The bodies were fed to zoo animals.

The white heron was the emblem of the Tlaxcalans.

Marina   Cortés   Montezuma

APPROACHING DOOM

When Cortés conquered the Tlaxcalan people, sworn enemies of the Aztecs, they joined his march to Tenochtitlan. As the army of 700 soldiers and 3,000 Tlaxcalans approached the city, Aztec princes met them and led them to the main gates, where Montezuma was waiting to greet them.

Montezuma and Cortés exchanged gifts of necklaces; the Spaniard's offering was made of glass beads, while the emperor's was pure gold.

THE ENEMY WITHIN

Montezuma knew these warriors could not be defeated in battle, so he treated them like gods. Meanwhile, they plotted his downfall.

CORTÉS FLEES THE CITY

The Aztecs were after Cortés's blood. When he tried to escape, they blocked his way by removing the drawbridges from the gaps in the main causeway. Cortes's men responded by building a portable bridge, but local women collecting water spotted them and alerted warriors, who launched an attack.

Aztec arrows killed hundreds of panicking Spaniards, but greed killed many more; laden with looted gold, they fell in the water and sank like stones.

THE SPANISH IN DEFEAT

Although Cortés survived, he lost half his own men and thousands of his native allies. The Spanish called this the Noche Triste (night of sorrow).

Active volcanoes fringed the lake basin.

Tenochtitlan teemed with people who came to worship, work in craft workshops, or trade in the markets. Food merchants sold a favorite delicacy – slugs with avocado dip.

THE EMPIRE GROWS, 1500

This community grew into a mighty city, Tenochtitlan (place of the cactus). By the beginning of the 16th century, its armies ruled an area as big as Great Britain, with five million inhabitants. While few were Aztec, they all had to pay taxes (called tribute) to the capital in the form of household goods, food, or trinkets. When they invaded a city, Aztec warriors took prisoners for sacrifice to their gods and captured thousands of young men, leaving the city too weak to fight.

Cortés

Cortés's native mistress, Marina, was his interpreter.

To make sure his troops would follow him, Cortés sank his own ships.

THE ENEMY APPEARS, 1519

Spanish soldiers led by Hernán Cortés arrived in 1519 to search for gold and spread Christianity. When he heard descriptions of Cortés, Montezuma mistook the Spaniard for the god Quetzalcoatl, who was thought to have a pale, bearded face. To welcome him, the emperor sent messengers bearing gifts.

INVADING FORCE

Despite this friendly welcome, the soldiers marched toward the capital, using steel weapons and firearms to overwhelm native armies on the way.

The natives had never seen horses, so at first they thought the mounted Spaniards were half human, half beast.

Tlaxcalan warrior

THE FALL OF MONTEZUMA, 1519

The Spanish took Montezuma hostage, making him a "puppet" ruler under their control. They looted his treasure and built a Christian altar on one of the pyramids. When soldiers massacred scores of religious revelers, the Aztecs finally fought back. Montezuma tried to intervene, but his people stoned him.

A MYSTERIOUS DEATH

Soon after his stoning, Montezuma was found dead. No one knows if he died from his injuries, or if the Spanish murdered him.

Aztec warrior

In the fierce fighting that followed the emperor's death, Spanish soldiers captured the Great Pyramid and burned the sacred shrines at the top.

Spanish standard (flag)

CORTÉS REGROUPS

Fleeing to the coast, Cortés trained more natives and built 13 new ships. His men took these to Lake Texcoco in pieces, then assembled them.

With both native and Spanish reinforcements, Cortés sailed across the lake. He and his men marched on the city of Tenochtitlan and slaughtered thousands of Aztecs.

END OF THE EMPIRE, 1521

The capital fell on August 13, 1521, and the rest of the empire soon followed. In less than a century, European diseases and brutal slavery slashed the population so that 19 out of every 20 natives died. The pride modern-day Mexicans feel for their Aztec past, however, is represented by the snake-eating eagle on their flag.

The Mogul Dynasty

THE GLITTERING MOGUL DYNASTY (ruling family) was founded in the 16th century by the Muslim warrior Babur, king of Kabul. Now capital of Afghanistan, Kabul was then part of the Persian Empire. From here, Babur invaded the northern part of India, which was mainly Hindu. Later, his descendants united the Indian people, expanding his kingdom to form a great power. The Mogul emperors ruled India from jewel-studded palaces, and their enormous wealth paid for some of the most beautiful paintings, literature, and buildings ever created.

At Panipat, Ibraham Lodi had more men and a team of war elephants.

Babur was still stronger, though, because he had experienced cavalry and his Turkish allies had supplied him with big guns.

INDIA INVADED, 1526
Fleeing from civil war, Babur looked southeast to India for a new empire. Though he was a skilled warrior, his first four raids ended in defeat. He won his fifth, the battle of Panipat, in 1526, even though he had 12,000 men, while his enemy Ibrahim Lodi, Sultan of Delhi, had more than 96,000.

BABUR TRIUMPHANT, 1526
After his victory, Babur moved on to Delhi and took the nearby city of Agra. The chiefs who controlled most of northern India, however, still opposed him. Babur was surrounded by enemies, and his troops, disheartened and suffering from the heat, wanted to go home.

Hindu temple

Akbar

THE GREATEST EMPEROR
Akbar's conquests doubled the area under Mogul rule and he controlled his lands shrewdly. He improved local government and supported the arts. Most importantly, Akbar ended the persecution of the Hindu people. He gave them important jobs and abolished special taxes, called *jizya,* on non-Muslims. When Akbar died in 1605, he was remembered for his strength, tolerance, and courage. Not everyone mourned him though, because he had a cruel streak, and lived in luxury while peasants starved.

Violence delighted Akbar. By organizing hunts before going to war, he showed his enemies what to expect if they opposed him. Tiger hunts were a particular favorite.

Shah Jahan

20,000 workers built the Taj Mahal.

Shah Jahan's son Aurangzeb

Mullahs (Muslim scholars)

Aurangzeb spent many hours in prayer.

MAGNIFICENT MONUMENT, 1632
One of the wonderful buildings Shah Jahan constructed was the white marble tomb known as the *Taj Mahal.* Intended as a memorial to his favorite wife Mumtaz Mahal, who died in 1631, the project was begun the following year and completed more than 20 years later.

THE LAST GREAT RULER, 1658
When Shah Jahan fell ill, his eldest son, Aurangzeb, imprisoned him and claimed the empire. To hold on to power, he ruthlessly executed two of his brothers. Aurangzeb's conquests of neighboring regions enlarged the empire. He was hardworking, educated, and intelligent – and a very devout Muslim.

Babur brought the culture of his homeland to India by building traditional Persian gardens.

A great poet as well as a great warrior, Babur dictated his memoirs to a scribe.

Akbar was only 20 when he got married in 1562, yet he had already ruled for seven years.

Akbar's bride was a Hindu princess. This match helped heal the rivalry between Muslims and Hindus, and won the support of rebellious Hindu chiefs.

LEADING BY EXAMPLE
To inspire his men, Babur poured away bottles of wine. (Although popular, wine was actually forbidden to Muslims.) Impressed by his devotion, his troops defeated another army at Khanua to the southeast. But peace escaped Babur. When he died in 1530, he left his son Humayan a land of fighting tribes.

THE AGE OF AKBAR, 1555
Humayan was weak, but his son Akbar – generous and wise, yet merciless to his enemies – strengthened the dynasty.

To celebrate a battle victory in 1560, Akbar built a great column. Before the building material had solidified, he had the heads of defeated soldiers embedded in its walls.

Jahangir gave away his weight in gold to the poor.

Shah Jahan's Peacock Throne

A WEAK RULER, 1605
When Akbar died, his son Jahangir became emperor. He carried on many of his father's good works, such as the Hindu practice of giving away his weight in gold and jewels annually. As he grew older, however, Jahangir lost interest in the empire. His wife and her family took control and ruled India.

SHAH JAHAN, 1627
When Jahangir died, no one was sure who should replace him. His third son, Shah Jahan, grabbed power, and to eliminate any rivals, he had one brother blinded and the others killed. After this violent start, his reign was peaceful. From his lavish palaces, he encouraged painting and literature, but his great love was architecture.

Aurangzeb ordered Hindu temples to be destroyed.

The tomb of Babur's son Humayan

A cattle cart hid the last emperor as British soldiers escorted him into exile.

THE DYNASTY FADES, 1707
Aurangzeb's strong religious feelings made him intolerant of Hindus. He reintroduced *jizya* taxes and destroyed Hindu schools and temples. His fierce encouragement of the Muslim faith made him very unpopular. After Aurangzeb died in 1707, the power of the Moguls faded and the British gradually gained control.

THE END OF THE LINE, 1857
The British *East India Company* began trading with India in the time of Jahangir. By the mid-19th century, it controlled most of India; the emperor, Bahdur Shah II, was powerless. In 1857 Indian soldiers mutinied against the British, who crushed the revolt and banished the emperor, ending the Mogul dynasty forever.

The Revolutionary War

FOR THE RIGHT TO LIFE, LIBERTY, and the pursuit of happiness, Americans fought a long revolutionary war. Settlers in 13 colonies along North America's east coast paid taxes to Britain, yet could not elect representatives to its Parliament. Anger over this flared into rebellion, then revolution — a violent struggle for political change. The 13 colonies began the war alone, but by 1780 France, Spain, and the Netherlands had offered support to the rebels. With their help, the colonists won, and the 13 colonies became one new nation, stretching from the Atlantic to the Mississippi River.

John Burgoyne

7. SARATOGA, 1777
Washington's daring attack across the Delaware ended the fighting for the winter. When it began again in 1777, the British were once more on the attack. They captured the colonial capital, Philadelphia, but didn't do as well farther north. At Saratoga colonial armies surrounded troops that had attacked from Canada. They forced British general John Burgoyne to surrender, on October 17. This victory helped persuade the French to recognize American independence. Four months later the French joined the war against Britain.

6. CROSSING THE DELAWARE, 1776
After the Declaration of Independence, the British acted to crush rebellion. Together with German hired soldiers, they drove George Washington's army from New York State, over the border at the Delaware River. But on Christmas night 1776, Washington led soldiers back across the frozen Delaware, and attacked an enemy camp at Trenton.

Washington's brilliant raid gave the revolutionaries badly needed encouragement.

Thomas Jefferson wrote most of the declaration.

Troops were half starved and their clothes were ragged.

George Washington

5. THE REVOLUTION BEGINS, 1776
Representatives of each colony had been meeting as the Continental Congress. The first Congress accepted rule by the British king, but did not believe Britain should make American laws. But when fighting began in 1775 Congress saw Britain planned to govern by force, and set up a provisional government to rule the 13 colonies as states. Later they chose complete freedom from Britain and set this out in a "Declaration of Independence," which Congress agreed upon in Philadelphia on July 4, 1776.

8. VALLEY FORGE, 1777-8
The colonial army camped for the winter of 1777-8 at Valley Forge, north-west of Philadelphia. Washington's exceptional leadership kept spirits up, and German officer Baron Friedrich Wilhelm von Steuben trained the troops. The tactics and discipline he taught the soldiers helped them defeat the British in the final years of the war.

Saratoga 1777

Saratoga

Trenton

Valley Forge *Philadelphia*

Philadelphia 1777

Delaware River

Yorktown 1781

Yorktown

Captain Marion was known as the "Swamp Fox" because after a raid his men would quickly disappear into the marshland.

Lord Cornwallis

9. THE BATTLE FOR THE SOUTH, 1780
Since neither side could win the war in the north, the British tried to conquer the southern states. By 1780 they controlled Georgia and South Carolina. Lord Cornwallis took command of the British troops. When he marched them into North Carolina and Virginia, colonial forces ambushed them everywhere. British control gradually weakened. French troops sailed to help the revolutionaries. In Virginia, Cornwallis made Yorktown his stronghold. But attacked there on land and sea, he had to surrender on October 19, 1781. When the British Prime Minister heard of the defeat, he cried, "Oh, God! It is all over!" The

10. SECURING VICTORY, 1781
In 1780, Charleston, South Carolina fell to the British, but many of its colonial defenders escaped capture. They gathered weapons and support, and began what we would now call guerrilla (little war) raids on the British. Many cunning raids were led by Captain Frances Marion, who became famous for his rescue of surrounded colonial troops at Parkers Ferry, South Carolina, in August 1781.

Parkers Ferry 1781

Parkers Ferry

Charleston

Paul Revere

Scarlet tunics gave the British redcoats their name.

2. REVERE'S RIDE, 1775

After the Boston Tea Party, the British tried to rule their rebellious colonies, and Massachusetts in particular, more firmly. Patriots (colonists opposed to British rule) did not like this interference, and they armed state militias (volunteer armies). When British troops marched from Boston on April 18, 1775, to destroy a weapons store at nearby Concord, patriot spies spotted them. Silversmith Paul Revere rode swiftly through the night to warn the militias of the danger.

Concord
Lexington and Concord 1775
Boston
Bunker Hill 1775

3. LEXINGTON AND CONCORD, 1775

Thanks to Paul Revere's ride, patriot troops were waiting for the British on the road to Concord. At Lexington, just outside Concord, British troops met 77 minutemen (patriot soldiers ready to fight at a minute's warning). In a confused battle, eight patriots died. When the British redcoats reached Concord, the arms they were seeking had been hidden, and they had to fight their way back to Boston.

The patriots were advised by their leader, John Parker, "... if they mean to have a war, let it begin here."

George Washington

Boston silversmith Paul Revere helped dump the tea.

Each chest of tea was worth a craftsman's wages for 18 months.

4. THE EVACUATION OF BOSTON, 1776

The battles of Lexington and Concord started the war. Soon afterward, hostile colonial soldiers besieged the British base in Boston. In June 1775 they occupied hills overlooking the port. British soldiers came to drive them off, but the patriots resisted. They killed or injured 1,000 redcoats in the battle of Bunker Hill. The siege ended when George Washington, commander of the colonial army, brought cannons to another hill overlooking the city. Rather than face bombardment, the British fled from Boston by ship on March 17, 1776.

1. THE "BOSTON TEA PARTY," 1773

Americans began resisting British taxation in 1765. Many taxes had been removed by 1773, but tea tax remained. Britain also tried to force Americans to buy tea from a British company, a move that would have put colonial merchants out of business. On December 16, 1773, a crowd protested in Boston, Massachusetts. Sixty people dressed as Native American Mohawks boarded British ships in the harbor and dumped 340 chests of tea overboard.

11. THE WAR AT SEA, 1781

Britain fought the colonists at sea as well as on land. It was an uneven battle: the British fleet was ten times the size of the colonial navy. When France and Spain entered the war, their powerful navies helped complete the defeat of the British.

In a battle off the Virginia Capes on September 5, 1781, the British fleet (right) was prevented from entering the Chesapeake Bay to relieve besieged troops in Yorktown by the French fleet (left) under the command of Admiral de Grasse.

The French Revolution

A VIOLENT UPHEAVAL SHOOK FRANCE at the end of the 18th century. The Age of Enlightenment had produced new ideas about life, religion, logic, and nature. In addition, France was facing a period of bad harvests and high prices. This led to demands for change in the way the king had control of the country. Early reforms produced a formal Declaration of the Rights of Man. Later, the monarchy was abolished, and France became a republic. Eventually though, violence ran out of control and discredited the Revolution.

Benjamin Franklin   *Extravagant queen Marie Antoinette dominated the king.*

AMERICAN THANKS, 1778

When the American colonies rebelled against Britain, France came to their aid. In 1778, American statesman Benjamin Franklin visited King Louis XVI to thank him. The Revolutionary War had been popular in France, but it cost a great deal and Louis had borrowed heavily to support it.

The members of the third estate assembled in the meeting hall of the king's palace at Versailles, near Paris.

KING CALLS ASSEMBLY, 1789

The king wanted to tax aristocrats, but only an elected national assembly with members from the three estates (aristocrats, clergy, and commoners) could pass such laws, so France held its first election in 175 years. The third estate (commoners) broke away, however, calling itself the National Assembly.

THE TENNIS-COURT OATH

The king responded by locking the third estate out of the meeting hall, so the Assembly met in the palace tennis court. Members swore not to disband until France had a new, fairer government to represent the people – not the king, church, and nobles. The nervous king agreed to some of their demands.

The women knew that the guards would not shoot them.

Exhausted after 24 hours on the road, the family did not resist capture.

WOMEN IN REVOLT, 1789

The Declaration of the Rights of Man made all Frenchmen equal. Women could not vote, but they still played an important part in the Revolution. On October 5, Parisian women angered by bread shortages marched 15 miles (23 km) to Versailles to demand that the king live in Paris. He meekly obeyed.

LOUIS ESCAPES, 1791

Intending to reach allies in Austria, Louis and his family fled Paris in disguise. But a post-master recognized them and alerted the authorities.

The king was dressed as a valet.

Guards arrested the royal family at Varennes, 125 miles (200 km) east of Paris, and took them back in disgrace.

Heads were collected in a basket.

"REIGN OF TERROR," 1793

The king's fate was sealed when papers were found at his palace that proved he had plotted against the Revolution. On January 21, 1793, he was executed. After this, the Revolution became more extreme. A radical leader, Maximilien Robespierre, took control, heading a Committee of Public Safety. His policies caused counterrevolutionary uprisings in much of France. The government responded with a "Reign of Terror," executing many thousands of its political opponents.

Most of the government's enemies were executed with a guillotine, which used a heavy, sharp blade to cut off people's heads quickly. The guillotine became a symbol of the Revolution.

Middle-class people had coaches and servants, but they wanted a share in government as well.

Peasant farmer

Castle

Oxen pulled the farmers' plows.

Church

Tax collector

AN UNEQUAL SOCIETY

The king was an absolute monarch, ruling with no elected government. The middle classes were wealthy, but they wanted power. Peasant farmers couldn't feed their families, yet they had to pay high taxes. They also paid high rents in money, produce, or labor to the aristocrats who owned the land. Yet these nobles in their castles paid no taxes, and opposed the king when he tried to make them pay. This situation produced simmering discontent.

Some peasants were also angry with the Catholic church, because they had no money to pay the tax collector, while bishops and cardinals lived in luxury.

The people took control of Paris.

Terrified aristocrats fled abroad.

STORMING THE BASTILLE, 1789

Nobody trusted the king. Louis believed he could keep power with help from the army, but he misjudged the mood of the people – a bad harvest had doubled bread prices so they were hungry and angry. On July 14, the citizens of Paris, supported by some police and soldiers, attacked the Bastille prison.

THE REVOLUTION SPREADS

The Revolution quickly spread out from Paris to other cities, and to the countryside, where four out of five French people lived.

Many peasants attacked their landlords' castles. Often their goal was to destroy the records that kept track of the hated taxes they were forced to pay.

Valmy was one of the first battles where massed artillery was used.

NERVOUS NEIGHBORS

The countries bordering France feared the Revolution might spread. Austria and Prussia plotted to restore Louis to the throne.

WAR IS DECLARED, 1792

As a result of this plot, France declared war on its two threatening neighbors. The revolutionary army beat off an invasion at the battle of Valmy five months later. This battle marked the beginning of a series of wars. At first the French people were fighting to defend the Revolution. The wars that followed, however, were fought simply to acquire more land. The French national anthem, the *Marseillaise*, was originally written as a call to arms for supporters of these wars.

Troops surrounded the city hall and captured Robespierrre.

Napoleon's armies were largely built up by conscription – forcing men to join.

THE TERROR GROWS, 1794

The Terror increased the following year as the revolutionaries defended their achievements. But Robespierre's methods made many enemies. The people began to turn against him. Faced with arrest, he hid in the Paris city hall. On July 28, he, too, was guillotined, and the Terror came to an end.

NAPOLEON ENDS THE REVOLUTION, 1795

In 1795, General Napoleon Bonaparte crushed a counterrevolution, and stability slowly returned. A military genius, Napoleon went on to increase France's power abroad. At home, he was made ruler in 1799, and emperor in 1804. His social reforms did much to create the France we know today.

Revolution in Russia

IN 1895, NICHOLAS II was crowned czar (emperor) of Russia. He believed his power came from God and called the idea of sharing government with the people a "senseless dream." In 1917, a revolution overthrew the czar, and in the confusion that followed, communists seized power. They believed everyone should share wealth equally. But the government they set up made life even harder for ordinary people. Russia's revolutionary experiment was not successful and lasted less than 75 years.

Nicholas   Rasputin

THE ROMANOV FAMILY
Romanovs had ruled Russia since 1613, but the people resented Nicholas and his family because of their pampered life. They were also suspicious of the wild-eyed monk Rasputin, whose apparent ability to heal the sick heir Alexis (born 1904) gave him control over the czar's wife, Alexandra.

The czar's Winter Palace was in St. Petersburg.

The worker's march included women and children. Some of them carried the czar's picture and icons (holy images).

WINTER PALACE MASSACRE, 1905
In 1905, a priest called Georgy Gapon led a protest march to the czar's Winter Palace. But troops fired on the peaceful crowd, killing over 100. This massacre triggered a revolt in the form of strikes, riots, and mutinies. It failed, but the czar agreed to some social reforms, which calmed unrest until World War I.

THE 1917 REVOLUTION
In 1914, Russia's entry into World War I revealed widespread government incompetence: their defeats were often due to lack of ammunition and food, and many people were hungry and freezing. In February 1917, soldiers joined the protests. The czar resigned and a Provisional Government took control.

The czar and his family were taken to a basement room to be shot.

DEATH OF THE ROMANOVS, 1918
In July 1918, White Russian troops advanced toward Yekaterinburg, where the Romanovs were prisoners. To prevent the family from being rescued, the local soviet (people's council) had everyone executed, including the doctor, servants, and dog. They burned the bodies and dissolved the bones in acid.

STALIN AND INDUSTRIALIZATION, 1929
Lenin's death in 1924 led to a long power struggle. By 1929, Joseph Stalin controlled the country, by this time called the Soviet Union. He built up industry and merged tiny farms into huge collectives. Stalin had millions of opponents imprisoned or killed, including Leon Trotsky.

Peasant farmers used simple tools to farm the land.

Lenin rouses his supporters with a passionate speech.

RUSSIA'S PEASANTS

Out of 130 million people, one third were serfs (near slaves) until 1861, when they were freed. But most were poor, and industry was undeveloped.

The peasants were deeply discontented because they had too little land to feed their families. Many drifted to cities, searching unsuccessfully for jobs.

LENIN PLOTS THE REVOLUTION, 1903

Discontent simmered and many people wanted revolution. But most revolutionary leaders had to flee abroad to escape the secret police. In 1903 one of them, Vladimir Ilich Lenin, founded a new party. From Switzerland, he planned to overthrow the czar and make Russia a communist state.

During the civil war, red army soldiers attacked many towns that were sympathetic to the counterrevolutionaries.

LENIN RETURNS, 1917

Lenin returned from exile by train through Germany. As Russia's enemy in World War I, Germany wanted Lenin to speed up Russia's surrender.

REVOLT AND CIVIL WAR

Lenin's revolutionaries, the Bolsheviks, seized power in October 1917, but they controlled only a small part of Russia. In a bitter civil war, an army of Bolsheviks – the Red Army, led by Leon Trotsky – fought the counter-revolutionary forces. Called White Armies, these were supported by foreign powers such as Britain, France, and the US. A two-year struggle, and a huge loss of life, led to a victory for the Bolsheviks, who later became the Communist Party.

Powers bailed out and was arrested.

The destruction of the Berlin Wall came to symbolize the fall of communism.

THE COLD WAR

The Soviet Union and the US were allies in World War II, but bitter rivals for power in the 1950s and 60s. This period is called the Cold War.

A high-flying American spy plane was shot down over Yekaterinburg at the height of political tension in 1960. Its pilot, Gary Powers, had been taking aerial photographs.

THE FALL OF SOVIET COMMUNISM, 1989

By the 1980s, people in the Soviet Union and its eastern European allies were demanding more freedom. In 1989, cheering crowds destroyed the Berlin Wall, a hated symbol of communism. Two years later, communist rule collapsed in the Soviet Union, ending the revolutionary experiment of 1917.

World War I

A CLUMSY ASSASSINATION in Sarajevo started the most appalling war the world had ever known. On June 28, 1914, a Serbian terrorist took aim at the governor of Bosnia. He missed, but instead killed Archduke Francis Ferdinand, prince of the empire of Austria and Hungary. The killing destroyed a fragile peace. Europe's nations had been forming alliances, hoping to expand their power and borders. Now they had an excuse to fight. By the time the war ended four years later, 14 million people had died.

German soldiers

Russian Cossack troops were noted cavalrymen.

GERMANY ADVANCES, 1914

In August, troops from Austria's ally Germany took Belgium. But at the battle of the Marne (September), British and French troops halted Germany's advance. To the east, however, at Tannenberg (now in Poland), Germany defeated a badly equipped army from Russia, ally of France and Britain.

British troops alone used more than ten million shovels during the war. Most of these were needed to dig trenches.

In World War I, combat aircraft were used for the first time.

THE WESTERN FRONT, 1915-18

After the Allies stopped the German advance at the Marne, both sides dug trenches. They defended them so well that further advances were impossible. For three years, millions of soldiers faced each other along the Western Front, a line of trenches from the English Channel to Switzerland.

TRENCH WARFARE

Mud, lice, and cold made life in the trenches almost unbearable. Deafened by shelling and choked by poisoned gas, many soldiers went mad.

Mud, often knee deep, filled the trenches, and rats grew fat from eating corpses. Snipers (hidden riflemen) made it dangerous to raise even a hand above the parapet.

GALLIPOLI

Both sides also looked for victory away from the Western Front. Troops from Britain, New Zealand, and Australia launched an attack on Turkey, but got trapped on the Gallipoli peninsula, on a vital shipping route between the Black and Mediterranean Seas. Before they could retreat 250,000 died.

DESERT WAR, 1917

The Allies feared Turkish capture of the Suez canal, which linked the Red and Mediterranean Seas. An Arab revolt against the Turks averted this.

English officer T.E. Lawrence disguised himself as an Arab and led the guerilla campaign against the Turks. His daring exploits made him a hero.

Lusitania

Zeppelins were as long as two city blocks.

LUSITANIA SUNK, 1915

In May 1915, a German submarine sank the British liner *Lusitania* off the Irish coast. Among the 1,400 passengers who died were 128

American citizens, including close friends of President Woodrow Wilson. The attack caused great anger in the United States. In 1917,

as a direct result of this and other attacks on neutral shipping, the US joined the war on the side of the Allies (France, Britain, and Russia).

BATTLING AIRSHIPS

Germany took the war to the air, dropping bombs on Britain from ten zeppelins – giant motorized airships. These raids killed 1,400 people.

High explosives were intended to destroy enemy trenches.

THE BATTLE OF THE SOMME, SUMMER 1916

Allied commanders launched an attack near the Somme River. Heavy guns shelled German trenches for a week, then Allied troops were ordered to *walk* toward enemy lines. That day, 20,000 Allied soldiers were killed; in all, 500,000 died. This slaughter moved the front line only 8 km (5 miles).

VERDUN, 1916

Some of the most bitter fighting of the war took place around Verdun Fort. 400,000 French were killed or hurt defending it from the Germans.

The strip between the trenches was called "no-man's land." It was usually about 250 yards (230 m) wide. Where troops were closer, they talked and sang with their enemy.

American soldiers join the Allied forces.

THE UNITED STATES JOINS THE ALLIES, 1917

When the US entered the war, they sent food and arms to England and France. But in spring 1918, before American troops could follow, Germany attacked on the Western Front. The Allies held them off, and a counterattack in the fall with American reinforcements forced Germany's surrender.

British engineers invented the tank to cross the mud of the Western Front. Although they helped win individual battles, tanks were unreliable, and contributed little to the final victory.

GERMANY SURRENDERS

War ended on November 11, 1918. In 1919, under the Treaty of Versailles, much of the land Germany gained was given back.

World War II

With Panzer tanks and Stuka dive bombers, the Germans mounted blitzkrieg (meaning lightning war) attacks.

DESPITE THE HORROR of World War I, the rumble of tanks and the drone of aircraft echoed across Europe again after just 21 years of peace. Partly to blame was the treaty that ended World War I, which imposed huge money and land penalties on Germany. Also, inflation in the 1920s made people's savings worthless, and the 30s Depression cost many their jobs. In their bitterness, they voted the Nazi (National Socialist) Party to power. Its leader, Adolph Hitler, became a dictator, crushing all opposition. The Allies – at first, France and Britain only – fought his plans to rule Europe.

GERMANY INVADES POLAND, 1939

After Hitler gained power in 1933, Germany built up its armies, taking control of Austria in 1938, then Czechoslovakia. But when Nazi troops invaded Poland in September 1939, Britain and France declared war. The following spring, German tanks swept through the Netherlands, Belgium, and France.

British tanks were less heavily armored than those of the Germans.

360 Japanese planes dive-bombed the unprepared American ships.

WAR IN THE DESERT

Italy, Germany's ally, declared war on Britain in 1940. In 1941, British troops in North Africa defeated the Italians, but they were driven back by reinforcements from Germany under General Rommel. The Allies did not regain Africa until 1943, when American troops arrived to support them.

PEARL HARBOR, 1941

The US joined the war after a surprise attack by Japanese aircraft on December 7, 1941, destroyed part of the American fleet at Pearl Harbor, Hawaii. The Japanese, hoping to conquer Southeast Asia, gambled on Allied forces in the Pacific being too weak to resist their ships and planes.

Flat-bottomed landing craft could anchor close to the beach. Each one carried 150 men.

During the first two days, 1,500 tanks landed. Fuel was pumped across the Channel in a special pipeline.

ALLIED PRESSURE GROWS, 1943

British and American troops advanced through Italy in 1943. Soviet forces drove the Germans back, winning massive tank battles. The Allies planned a definitive end to the war in Europe; they prepared to mount a huge invasion of France from Britain, while aircraft bombed German forces in France.

D-DAY INVASION, 1944

The attack, on the northern French coast, came on June 6, known as D-Day. By August, the Allies had liberated the French capital, Paris.

More than a million British, Canadian, and American troops landed in France within three weeks of D-Day. The soldiers faced fierce German resistance.

Bombing destroyed Dunkirk's harbor, so large ships could not dock.

Instead, a fleet of small boats sailed from England to rescue the troops.

Spitfires were the fastest fighters flying, and radar directed pilots to incoming bombers. Britain's allies supplied some of the best pilots, such as the Pole Joseph Frantisek.

DUNKIRK RETREAT, 1940
In northern France, German troops surrounded Allied forces. In May, the British and French retreated across the English Channel from Dunkirk.

THE BATTLE OF BRITAIN, 1940
The German air force (the *Luftwaffe*), under Herman Goering, intended to pave the way for an invasion of England by destroying the Royal Air Force. But in spectacular air battles during the summer of 1940, British fighters shot down waves of German bombers, foiling the planned attack.

American planes sank four Japanese aircraft carriers.

750,000 Soviet soldiers died defending their city in fierce house-to-house fighting.

BATTLE OF MIDWAY, 1942
In June 1942, the United States dramatically halted Japan's advance in the Pacific during the battle for an American naval base on the island of Midway. This was one of the first sea battles to be fought entirely by aircraft.

STALINGRAD, 1942
Hitler signed a pact with the Soviets, but when he later attacked their country, they joined the Allies. At Stalingrad, the Soviets defeated the Germans, who lost 110,000 men from their army of 270,000.

CONCENTRATION CAMPS
During the war, the Nazis killed six million Jews and many other people at camps such as Auschwitz, in German-occupied Poland.

"Winnie" (Winston Churchill) raised two fingers in his famous V-for-victory salute.

On August 6, the world's first atomic bomb was dropped on Hiroshima from a bomber named Enola Gay after the pilot's mother.

BERLIN CAPTURED, 1945
While Allied troops liberated the lands taken by Germany, their leaders, Churchill, Roosevelt, and Stalin, met at Yalta to discuss the division of Europe after the war. When Soviet troops entered the German capital, Berlin, Hitler killed himself.

VE DAY, 1945
Germany surrendered on May 8, 1945. On this "Victory in Europe" (VE) day, London crowds mobbed the British war leader Winston Churchill.

VJ DAY, 1945
The Japanese emperor, Hirohito, surrendered on August 15 (VJ Day), after the Americans dropped atomic bombs on the cities of Hiroshima and Nagasaki.

INDEX

A

Agincourt, battle of, 17
Akbar, Emperor, 20, 21
Alexander the Great, 89
Alexius, Emperor, 14, 15
Antioch, 15
atomic bomb, 31
Aurangzeb, Emperor, 20
Aztecs, 18-19

B

Babur, Emperor, 20
Babylon, 8
barbarians, 11
Bastille, 25
Berlin, 31
Berlin Wall, 27
Black Prince, 16
Bolsheviks, 27
Boston Tea Party, 23
Britain, battle of, 31

C

Calais, 16, 17
Carthage, 10
Charles the Mad, king of
    France, 17
Charles the Wise, king of
    France, 17
Charles VII, king of
    France, 16, 17
Churchill, Winston, 31
Cibotus, 14
Cold War, 27
communism, 26, 27
concentration camps, 31
Concord, battle of, 23
Constantinople, 12, 14
Cortés, Hernán, 18, 19
Crécy, battle of, 17
Crusades, 14-15

D

D-Day invasion, 30
Darius III, king of Persia, 8, 9
Declaration of Independence, 22
Delaware River, 22
desert wars, 28, 30
Dunkirk, 31

E

East India Company, 21
Edward III, king of England,
    16, 17
Egypt, 6-7, 8, 10
England, 10, 12-13, 16-17

F

France, 16-17, 22, 23, 24-25,
    28, 29, 30
French Revolution, 24-25
Francis Ferdinand, Archduke, 28
Franklin, Benjamin, 24

G

Gallipoli, battle of, 28
Germany, 28-29, 30-31
Giza, 6
gladiators, 11
Great Britain, 22-23, 24, 28, 29,
    30, 31
guillotine, 24

H

Hadrian's Wall, 10
Hannibal, 10
Harald the Ruthless, king of
    Norway, 13
Hastings, battle of, 13
Henry V, king of England, 17
Hitler, Adolf, 30, 31
Holy Land, 14
Horatius, 10
Hundred Years War, 16-17

I

India, 9, 20-21
Issus, battle of, 8
Italy, 30

J

Jahangir, Emperor, 21
Japan, 30, 31
Jefferson, Thomas, 22
Jerusalem, 14
Joan of Arc, 16, 17
Julius Caesar, 10

K

Khufu, Pharaoh, 67

L

Lawrence of Arabia, 28
Lenin, Vladimir Ilich, 27
Lexington, battle of, 23
Lindisfarne, 12
Loire River, 16, 17
longships, 13
Louis XVI, king of France,
    24, 25
Lusitania, 29

M

Macedonia, 8
Marne, battle of, 28
Marseillaise, 25
Mexico, 18-19
Midway, battle of, 31
Montezuma, Emperor, 18, 19

N

Napoleon Bonaparte, 25
National Assembly, 24
Nazi Party, 30
Nero, Emperor, 11
Newfoundland, 13
Nicholas II, czar of Russia, 26
Nile River, 6-7, 8

O

Octavian, Emperor, 11
Orléans, battle of, 17

P

Pearl Harbor, 30
Persia, 8
Peter the Hermit, 14-15
pharaohs, 6
Poitiers, battle of, 16
Poland, 30
pyramids, 6-7, 18

R

Rasputin, 26
Reign of Terror, 24, 25
Revere, Paul, 23
Revolutionary War, 22-23, 24
Robespierre, Maximilien, 25
Roman Empire, 10-11
Romanovs, 2
Romulus and Remus, 10
Russia, 12, 28, 29
Russian Revolution, 26-27

S

Saratoga, battle of, 22
Seine River, 16, 17
Shah Jahan, 21
ships, 7, 13, 15
Sluys, battle of, 17
Somme, battle of, 29
Somme River, 17
Soviet Union, 26-27
Spaniards, 18-19
Spartacus, 11
Stalin, Joseph, 2
Stalingrad, 31

T

Taj Mahal, 20
tanks, 29, 30
Tennis-Court Oath, 24
Tenochtitlan, 18, 19
trench warfare, 28, 29
Trotsky, Leon, 26, 27
Turkey, 14, 15, 28
Tutankhamen, 7
Tyre, siege of, 8

U

United States, 22-23, 27, 29,
    30, 31
Urban II, Pope, 14

V

Valmy, battle of 25
VE and VJ Day, 31
Verdun, battle of, 29
Versailles, Treaty of, 29, 30
Vikings, 12-13
Visigoths, 11

W

Washington, George, 22, 23
William the Conqueror, 13
Winter Palace massacre, 26
World War I, 26, 28-29
World War II, 27, 30-31

Y

Yalta, 31

Z

zeppelins, 29

ACKNOWLEDGMENTS

DK would like to thank the following for
helping with this book:

Design: Joanne Earl, Mark Haygarth,
Joanna Pocock

Editorial: Francesca Baines, Reg Grant,
Nancy Jones, Nigel Ritchie

Index: Chris Bernstein

Research: Charles Burns, Amanda
Claridge, Chris Daniell, Robert Graham,
R.E. Howard-Malverde, Dr Simon James,
Angela Koo, Divia Patel, James Putnam.